MW00681395

Best Advice on
STARTING A HAPPY MARRIAGE

Foreword by STACIA RAGOLIA

RUTLEDGE HILL PRESS™

Nashville, Tennessee

A DIVISION OF THOMAS NELSON, INC.
www.ThomasNelson.com

Published by Rutledge Hill Press, a Division of Thomas Nelson, Inc., P.O. Box 141000, Nashville, Tennessee 37214.

Library of Congress Cataloging-in-Publication Data

Best advice on starting a happy marriage / foreword by Stacia Ragolia.
    p. cm. — (iVillage Solutions)
Excerpts from online discussions on the iVillage.com web site.
ISBN 1-4016-0097-2
1. Marriage. I. Series
HQ734.B615 2003
306.81—dc21

2003005206

Printed in the United States of America

03 04 05 06 07 — 5 4 3 2 1

CONTENTS

Other Books from iVillage Solutions

Best Advice on Finding Mr. Right
Best Advice on Life After Baby Arrives
Heirloom Recipes
Quiz Therapy

FOREWORD

By Stacia Ragolia

In my early twenties, before I myself wed, a friend of mine received a pair of Indonesian marriage dolls as a wedding gift. Traditionally, these dolls are placed outside the door of a couple's house for the first year of their marriage. When the dolls are set next to each other, shoulder to shoulder and facing outward in the same direction, those visiting know that there is harmony in the house. How powerful, I thought—defining marital happiness not as gazing into each other's eyes but looking out toward the same horizon.

That every couple embarking on a marriage hopes it will be a happy one is a given. But making that a reality stymies at least half of all couples who say, "I do;" as the oft-quoted statistics show, about one in every two marriages ends in divorce. This book presents lessons from the other side of those numbers. The women who have contributed their advice to this book have, collectively, navigated hundreds of years of happy marriage. They represent the 50 percent who *stay together*.

Like that older sister or aunt who has a few years of marriage under her belt and pulls you aside at the wedding reception to impart some of her advice, the women whose insights and solutions make up this book are here to give you pointers as you set out on an adventure we all hope will last your entire life.

None of these women will pretend that arguments don't occur, challenges don't arise, or setbacks don't crop up. Having a happy marriage, they'll tell you, is not about avoiding problems, but learning how to deal with them — together. Whether the issue at hand is a depleted bank account, how to raise the kids (or even whether to have any), or whose turn it is to load the dishwasher, a couple needs to come at the situation with the belief that they're ultimately on the same side. As one woman puts it, "You are a team, living together as a unit. Treat your spouse the way you would want to be treated. No one is perfect. Address problems, learn from mistakes, and always look toward the future."

Which brings us to some other powerful lessons happy couples know. You can deal with today's problems if you base your actions on a belief that tomorrow you'll still be together. Treating your spouse with respect helps you deal with situations rationally. And finally, a sense of humor helps turn even the worst moment around. "My spouse and I have always agreed that we'd rather die laughing than live sadly," relates one of our contributors. "It's much easier to get past a bad joke than it is to take back hurtful words once spoken." So do I have a happy marriage? Yes, I have to say I do. Seven years, two kids, and a house later, there have been plenty of times I haven't agreed with my husband, but there has been no situation that we've encountered that we didn't feel we could handle together — and handle better together than we could on our own, by facing outward, looking toward the same future.

PREFACE

Since iVillage was founded in 1995, thousands of women have come to the discussion groups on the web site in search of advice about relationships. In dozens of groups devoted to tackling the issues that arise in the course of a marriage, they've found other women who gladly share their tips with a big helping of friendship and support. In this book, you'll find the very best solutions women have shared with each other on iVillage.

iVillage would like to thank the members of iVillage.com's Relationships channel (www.ivillage.com/relationships) for sharing their words of wisdom and inspiration. Without them this book would not exist. We'd also like to thank the hundreds of community leaders who host our online discussion and support groups for the care, concern, and support they provide to our members. Patricia Timmermans provided invaluable assistance in helping us gather advice from the members of the iVillage community. And finally, many thanks to Carmela Ciuraru for translating those many strains of online conversation into this book.

CHAPTER 1

How to Stay in Love

"Hug and kiss each other every day. And no matter how long you've been married or how busy your schedules are, never stop going out on regular dates, just the two of you. It will sustain your attraction and make it even stronger over time."

LEARN TO LIKE, NOT JUST LOVE, EACH OTHER

"There are some obvious things that keep couples together, communication and honesty among them. But my husband and I believe that it isn't enough to love one another—you have to like one another too! Have some common interests, and enjoy each other's company."

" *If* you don't have admiration for each other, things will not work. Don't let anything get in the way of respecting each other. Growing old together means exactly that, so accept that the body will change and love the person for who he is inside. "

"*Because* passion might fizzle out, and it's hard to feel loving when you experience hard times, you are going to need friendship. You should like and appreciate your husband even when you don't feel romantic. Few marriages can be sustained without friendship. My husband and I are best friends and soul mates, and I treasure that always."

"We all love that giddy, I-can't-live-without-you phase every relationship has in the beginning. Just because that phase doesn't last forever, it doesn't mean you don't love each other any more; it just means reality has set in."

"Learn to truly like your spouse as a person. Passion waxes and wanes, romance can come and go, but genuine, deep respect for your partner will carry you through good and bad times."

TREAT EACH OTHER WITH RESPECT

"Respecting each other means appreciating each other's best qualities, which is something that builds over time. You have to learn to show respect even when the chips are down, not just in happy times."

"*I* wouldn't have stayed married for thirty years if my husband didn't respect me. And it goes both ways. Of course there are always things we wish we could change about each other, but these are things we have learned to live with — or they are things we are both still working on. You always need to be patient with each other."

"Respect, both giving it and getting it, allows you to communicate and be honest about things, even when it's a touchy subject. When you do argue or disagree, do so with a certain amount of respect for the other's opinions and feelings. Really listen to what your spouse is saying, and ask questions to help clarify your understanding of his points instead of assuming you know what he 'really' means."

"Treating each other with respect means knowing that, no matter what, someone always 'has your back.' That kind of respect sustains and builds passion over time. Few things are more attractive than knowing you are respected by your spouse, and feeling and expressing compassion for each other."

"Respecting your spouse means (among other things) never forgetting to use your best manners. Say 'please,' 'thank you,' 'excuse me,' 'I appreciate you,' 'how are you today?' and so on. We all want to be treated kindly, especially by those we choose to be with for a lifetime."

LAUGH WITH EACH OTHER

"Laugh as often as you can, especially when the going gets tough. You can't hold onto anger when you are laughing. Even when we argue, one of us usually says something in the heat of the moment that is so stupid that the other starts to laugh. End of argument."

"My husband and I find comfort in our familiarity with each other. Lots of personal jokes and memories mean that we can carry on some strange conversations and know exactly what the other is talking about. We've found a sense of humor to be a priceless commodity. Humor has helped lighten many a mood and has often put an already good day over the top."

"My spouse and I have always agreed that we'd rather die laughing than live sadly. Laughter is always, ultimately, the best response—and truly the best medicine, no matter what the problem or cause of conflict. It's much easier to get past a bad joke than it is to take back hurtful words once they are spoken."

"I think one of the best things in the world is laughter. If you can be silly with your spouse and act like two-year-olds together—be each other's best friend—you've got a great foundation to work upon."

" *I* knew that my husband was 'the one' when I noticed (while we were still dating) that he laughed at my jokes all the time, and I at his. It was such a relief. I thought, 'Finally, someone who understands my jokes and shares my sense of humor!' Now I can always feel secure knowing there is at least one person in the world who fundamentally 'gets' me. Of course, a successful marriage is made up of many things, but for us, humor is an integral part of the relationship, and it keeps us from getting too serious in life. "

KEEP ON DATING

"We have held onto our courtship rituals, like romantic dinners, long talks, bicycle riding, going out dancing, and exchanging gifts, even when there is no 'real' occasion. Those rituals have strengthened our bonds of intimacy. If you come up with some rituals of your own and stay committed to them, passion and attraction will be with you for the long haul."

"*F*ind an activity (outside of the bedroom) that just the two of you can enjoy together. For my husband and me, it's ballroom dancing. It's kind of like long-term dating!"

"*H*aving a date on a regular basis is a great way to reconnect, no matter how busy you are. Sometimes that means putting your foot down, calling a babysitter, and just going out and enjoying an evening alone with your husband."

"When my husband and I go out on dates, I try to dress in a sexy way because I think that's what attracted my husband in the first place. He also liked my spontaneity and my ability to cut loose and have a good time. So I try to return to that mindset for our date nights. And we always manage to have fun and have time just to be a couple, without talking about the kids."

"*Even* if a date night can't happen every week, arranging special time together is important to do when you can. There are many things that bring a couple together, and those things shouldn't be lost in the shuffle of daily life and parenthood."

STAY PASSIONATE

"If possible, set aside special time every day for
getting reacquainted. Maybe it's just fifteen
minutes at night before you go to bed. This can be
tons of fun. Leave notes on each other's pillows,
take showers together—whatever seems like an
exciting way to spend time together."

"*D*espite our hectic schedules, my husband and I always find time for even the slightest gestures—a smile, a touch, a quick kiss. He always makes a point of touching me if we're in the same room, just to feel close and make a connection."

"*K*iss and hug each other every day. Stay physically affectionate with each other. It will enrich your communication and make you both feel loved."

"*C*all each other at a certain time of the day, just to check in and say a quick 'I love you.' Read aloud together. Write each other love letters. And always greet each other (affectionately) when you get home from work."

"After nine years of marriage, my husband and I stay passionate by staying young at heart. We go out at a moment's notice, and we sing silly songs while driving. We also have a 'lovin' room' in the house: a spare room that we decorated as a hotel room, complete with a mini-fridge and bar. When we close the door to this room, we feel like we are the only two people in the world. We also have a hot tub on our deck and love taking late-night dips under the moonlight."

BUILD TRADITIONS AS A COUPLE

"Breakfast in bed every Saturday morning is a tradition that began while we were still dating and is one we still keep up, no matter what. It's a great way to feel connected after a long, busy, and exhausting week at work, and it's a wonderful way to begin each weekend."

"One Valentine's Day my husband completely
surprised me by driving me to a B&B overnight.
Ever since then, we've made it a tradition,
returning to the same place and staying in the same
room each year. It's a special ritual that we always
look forward to and one that allows us to pamper
ourselves together."

"Every year, around my birthday, we take off for two days in the middle of the week. We go to a romantic spot within a few hours' drive of our house. We rent a room with a hot tub in it, and if the hotel offers a 'romance' package, we take it! It gives us a chance to unwind and recharge our batteries."

"Some friends gave us a beautiful scrapbook with a clipping in it that tells a story of growing old and watching your lives unfold together. The story basically tells you to take a picture of each other on every anniversary and include it in the scrapbook. That way you can look back after several years of marriage and see the transitions you experienced together."

"*I* love traditions, but since my family had few to speak of, I decided to start my own when I got married. So for our first wedding anniversary, I surprised my husband by beginning a new tradition. At dinner that evening, I handed my husband a journal. Inside I had written about the memories (accompanied with silly drawings) I thought best reflected our year together. At the end of the entries, I included a review about a special bottle of wine I'd bought for us to share. Now, every year we each add our most important memories of the year to the journal and read them together over dinner on our anniversary, and then we choose the bottle of wine to add to our growing collection. I love that we don't fuss over buying each other expensive gifts because nothing could compare to the tradition we've created around this special day."

CHAPTER 2

How to Communicate

⌒

"For a marriage to be happy and long lasting, you really have to enjoy being with your spouse—and most importantly, enjoy talking with him."

RECOGNIZE (AND WORK WITH) YOUR DIFFERENT STYLES OF COMMUNICATION

"*I* am a hot-tempered woman, and my husband is a pretty quiet and mellow guy. So he knows not to attack me with accusations or harsh words, which would make me fly off the handle. He stays calm when I gripe. Constructive criticism is really the best way to handle any issue. It prevents a problem from escalating and becoming unmanageable."

"*A*llow equal time for each of you to be the talker and the other to just be the listener. That way, you'll both have your say rather than one person dominating the conversation, which is not productive."

"*I*f something is troubling me, I put pen to paper to identify where my feelings are coming from. My husband might not write things down like I do, but he will help me by reading what I have written. We use this writing to start a dialogue, addressing point by point what the concerns are. We've learned to value the uniqueness of what we each bring to the table."

"*A*fter you get married, you may feel more comfortable griping about things you didn't feel free to say earlier in the relationship. Speaking freely is great, but think about how important something is, how much it really gets on your nerves, before expressing your gripe. If your spouse is the one who tends to do the complaining and sometimes you feel it's uncalled for, try to stay calm rather than overreacting. Learn to understand each other's ways of expressing hurt or annoyance, and be patient if those responses differ from one another."

"When we first got married, my husband and I got off to a shaky start. We had plenty of conflicts as a couple and different ways of talking about them. What really strengthened our relationship was attending a series of couples' communications classes together. A decade later we still use the rules that we learned in those classes, and it has made a world of difference for us."

ACKNOWLEDGE THAT YOU'LL HAVE DIFFERENCES OF OPINION

"Even in the happiest marriages, two people are bound to disagree. On issues that don't affect our daily lives, my husband and I pretty much agree to disagree. That's one great aspect of our relationship. We are able to discuss topics on which we hold fundamental differences of opinion without getting into an argument. We know that we won't agree, but sometimes it's fun to discuss these things (such as political or religious views). On things that we must agree on, like how to raise our kids, we always discuss them and arrive at a compromise. That way there is no resentment. We just stay calm and always find a way."

"It isn't always necessary to talk things out when you disagree. I used to be the kind of person who wanted to work out a dispute at all costs. But now I find that the best solution to a disagreement is often to 'sleep things off.' That way you can decide in the morning, after a good night's rest, whether to pick the subject up where you left off, or to put the matter behind you—and simply agree to disagree."

"Although you might disagree sometimes, never undermine your spouse in front of others. Remember that you are a team! Support and cheer each other in everything that you do in life."

"When people don't like their spouses to speak their minds, that usually indicates they are insecure. When one of you disagrees with the other's opinions, you might feel threatened if you think absolute agreement on everything is necessary in a marriage. Talk about expectations with your husband: Does he understand that, even though you don't always agree, you still love each other? Do you? Make sure you have similar ideas about your partnership, and reassure each other that occasional differences of opinion are fine."

"When we have a difference of opinion, we usually just tell each other why we think we are right. And sometimes one of us actually has a point the other person hadn't thought of. But when we don't agree, it's not a big deal, so we just let things lie. If it isn't a major issue for me, I usually let it go. We both realize that we can't change each other, and we accept that."

*F*IGHT FAIR

"*A*lways find the right time—for both of you—
to discuss things. If you need to explain to your
husband that you need some time to collect your
thoughts, do so. And after you have talked things
through (in a nonaccusatory way), find some
common ground on which to end the discussion,
even if you don't totally agree."

"Whenever one of us is angry, we talk it out or give each other space to cool off. We don't add fuel to the fire with provocation—we don't bring up mistakes of the past. And we never disrespect each other, no matter what happens."

"Think about creating a list of five to ten ground rules that you will both adhere to in a disagreement. When one of you feels one of those rules has been violated, call a five-minute 'time out' to cool things off."

"*D*on't be afraid to argue, but do it respectfully. Stick to the issues rather than making personal attacks, and learn to negotiate and compromise. Honest but constructive arguments will actually strengthen your marriage in the long run."

"*If* you need to express unhappiness about something your husband has done, don't load your remarks with blame. As soon as you do that, he will either shut down and stop listening or become defensive and he won't respond in the way you'd like. Also, never frame things in an accusatory way because that won't help either of you."

BEING RIGHT ISN'T EVERYTHING

"Sometimes, even when you know it's time to step out for a walk after a disagreement, you still feel a need to prove that you're right. My husband and I have realized that often we are both wrong. So before we say things we might regret, we take time to give each other space and cool off. We never hold on to the need to be 'right' about something. And sometimes we even forget what started the disagreement in the first place."

"Picking your battles is a good lesson to learn, especially if you plan to have children. There are many things I would rather just live with than spend each day fighting about; it's just not worth it, and fighting doesn't do either of us any good."

"Part of the secret to a happy marriage is knowing when to let go. It's all about talking yet respecting your partner's limits. Sometimes it means letting him get his way. Hopefully he will do the same for you sometimes. You should both keep an open mind about everything and be able to admit when you're mistaken. Marriage is give and take, and tolerating and forgiving."

"*L*earn to let go of the small things. Save your arguments for what really matters. If you argue about petty issues, you'll never get past those to take care of the big things."

"*I*f your goal is to achieve a solution to a problem, then two heads really are better than one. But if one person always has to be right, then the problem will just continue. Put the egos aside."

LEARN HOW TO MAKE UP

"Sometimes one of you will behave like a creep. Remember that romance, and making up after a fight, is not just about flowers or sweet talk. Do thoughtful, practical things for your spouse to show you're sorry or that you care: Wake up with a smile for him, pick up a special treat for him at the grocery store, or fill up the gas tank when you know he'll be pressed for time. And share a laugh. Humor is infectious as long it is good-natured and not used to ridicule."

"*Y*ou are a team, living together as a unit. Treat your spouse the way you would want to be treated. No one is perfect. Address problems, learn from mistakes, and always look toward the future. Remember that you are best friends."

"*N*ever go to bed angry or leave the house without saying, 'I love you.' Never take that for granted. If there's a dispute about something minor, don't get too caught up in it. Take time out, cuddle up, and watch a movie."

"My husband and I have always had a deep and abiding love, and that has helped us make up after any situation, big or small. Just go into your marriage with the idea that you will always make it, no matter what. It works."

"*M*ake up by simply forgiving each other. Sometimes that means both of you should apologize, but sometimes it just means one of you taking the initiative and saying, 'I love you. I forgive you. Let's go spend some time together.' It's about working things through, putting the disagreement behind you right away, and moving on."

CHAPTER 3

How to Handle the Tough Stuff

"Once we got married, my husband and I began to focus on building a life together and on all our new responsibilities. We had a rocky time negotiating many of the issues. Despite that, we were dedicated to making our marriage work and learned to work together and trust each other. Being married is the hardest thing I have ever done but also the most rewarding. And it has gotten much easier over time."

*A*FFAIR-PROOF YOUR MARRIAGE

"*I*f your spouse sometimes engages in what you feel is inappropriate behavior, such as flirting, sit down and let him know that you feel hurt and embarrassed. Both of you need to establish boundaries early on about what is acceptable behavior. If one of you does feel threatened in some way, be sure to validate each other's feelings and reaffirm your love."

"*O*ccasionally people let their imaginations get the best of them and project everything they think they want from their spouse, but aren't getting, onto someone else. If you find yourself entertaining an infatuation, pull yourself back and redirect your energy back into your marriage. You'll be glad you did."

"*T*alk about what you consider infidelity and what makes you feel threatened, so that there can be no misunderstanding. Sometimes cheating can be an emotional pull rather than just a physical act, so it's essential that if you feel unhappy about anything, you discuss it immediately. Work things out before they seem insurmountable. Turn to each other, rather than someone outside the marriage, to face problems and get what you want."

"Never use sex as a weapon in a dispute with your spouse—for instance, withholding sex as a way of dealing with an issue that's troubling you. Always keep the lines of communication open. If they shut down, you might want to consider counseling. There are various stages of love in a marriage, so be prepared for your love (and intimacy) to keep shifting over time. Both of you should realize that change is not a reason to look for sexual fulfillment outside of the marriage."

"It's easy for anyone to be tempted occasionally. But realizing the consequences and pain that giving in to that temptation would cause—not only to yourself but the loved one you'd betray—is a great deterrent. I've been married for nearly six years, and it hasn't all been a bed of roses, but every obstacle we deal with together makes us stronger. Neither of us would go outside of our marriage to another person. Although we never consciously 'affair-proofed' our relationship, we were secure in our beliefs about fidelity before we married—and we have not forgotten the promises we made to each other at our wedding."

COPE WITH PHYSICAL SEPARATIONS

"The first time one of you has to go away for an
extended period (whether it be for business, a
family visit, or an emergency) may be the hardest
to deal with. Talk about how you'll stay connected
before the trip, and be creative. That should
alleviate your anxiety, and you could even plan
a special night together after you or your spouse
returns."

"While your spouse is away, try to get out of the way some mundane tasks that you haven't had time to do. That way you can look forward to quality time when he returns. And schedule time with friends so you won't feel as lonely."

"Separation is tough, but it might offer the perfect opportunity for you to pamper yourself! Rent movies, cook your favorite meal, have a bubble bath, go shopping, order takeout, catch up with friends, write in a journal. That doesn't mean you won't miss your spouse, but solitude can allow you to do things you normally don't have time to do. And if you have children, set some time aside for special activities, such as going to a museum or zoo or taking a day trip together."

"My husband travels a lot for his job, which is always hard. I like to plan big homecomings for him. Once I placed a small candle on every step of the staircase leading up to our bedroom. Another time I had a big picnic dinner spread out in the middle of the living room waiting for him. I also love to pack cards in his suitcase and little things for him to unwrap each day that he's gone. He loves that! I certainly don't look forward to his absences, but I do try to make the most of the time I have while he is away."

"When you are apart, talk on the phone every night before you go to sleep. My husband is often out of town on business, and it's comforting to have his voice be the last thing I hear every evening. Sometimes we check in a few times a day by phone, which can get expensive, but it's worth it. Another thing I like to do is send my husband something that lets him know I'm thinking about him, such as homemade cookies. And sometimes I spice things up by sending him sexy lingerie and telling him that when he returns, I'll wear it for him."

$\mathcal{D}$ISCUSS HOW YOU FEEL ABOUT CHILDREN

"$\mathcal{I}$t's important to discuss having children, not only before you get married but also as an ongoing dialogue after you get married. My husband and I talked about becoming parents while we were still dating. We both knew we wanted children and even agreed on the number. After our third child was born, however, my husband approached me with the idea of not having any more. After a year of thinking about it and discussing it, we came to the conclusion that we were both happy to stop our family at three kids, although we'd originally wanted five. As with everything in marriage, communication is key."

"Make sure you're both completely comfortable with your decision about whether to have children. Be honest with yourself. I married a man who already had children from his first marriage and who absolutely didn't want more. Had I married someone else, I would have had kids without hesitation, but instead I chose to be with my soulmate. It took me a long time to become comfortable with my decision to forfeit kids. I worried that people would think I was selfish or that I would feel incomplete. Thankfully, I am now happy with my decision and have no regrets. If you do want kids, make sure you both truly want them and that you're not doing it simply because you think you should."

"It's a good idea to stay flexible in your thinking about children because life changes. When we first got married, my husband and I had decided that we'd wait at least five years before having children. However, as our arbitrary deadline approached, we both realized that we didn't really want to change our lifestyle to accommodate children after all. Luckily we're 'on the same page' about remaining childless, but I'm willing to stay open-minded, as is my husband."

"Neither my husband nor I wanted children, but when I first met him, he was convinced that it was just something you had to do. He felt guilty about his desire to remain childless. Early on we discussed this issue often and even went to a counselor to be absolutely sure that we were comfortable not having children. It helped us tremendously, and now we both feel secure in our decision."

"My husband is older than I and has an adult daughter by a previous marriage; his initial feeling about having children was that he didn't want to start over. We got some counseling right before we married, and it really helped him figure out his specific fears about starting a new family, which in turn helped me understand him better. He never once argued against my reasons for wanting a child. He said he understood why I wanted a child. But yet he couldn't just take the plunge. It got to the point where we were having a 'baby discussion' once a month. When I was able to control the emotional component on my part, the discussions improved and I saw some light at the end of the tunnel. Finally he agreed to try to conceive, and a month later I was pregnant. We're expecting our first in just a few months."

TALK ABOUT HOW TO RAISE THE KIDS (IF YOU DECIDE TO HAVE THEM)

"If your spouse has children from a previous marriage, determine what your role will be in regard to them and make sure you are both comfortable with it. Will you be more of a friend or mentor to them? Should you discipline them when appropriate? How comfortable are the children with accepting you as a parental figure? Discuss all of this so that no one ends up feeling hurt or undermined."

" *F*igure out in advance how you will handle child care. Establish these responsibilities in a way that is satisfactory to both you and your spouse so that neither of you feels resentful later on. "

" *M*y husband and I have very different approaches to raising our children. He often lets bad behavior slip by, as he'd rather not deal with it, which means it's usually up to me to set punishments. He tends to retreat in the face of conflict; my style is to meet it head on. I don't mind being the 'bad cop' as long as I get his support. "

"Make sure you are both on the same page about public school versus private school. Both of you want a great education for your kids, but one of you might want to have a religious component in their schooling. Research all the options until you both feel happy about the children's school environment."

"My husband and I come from two different religious backgrounds. He's Jewish; I'm Catholic. We talked early on—in fact, even before our marriage—about how we wanted to see our children raised in light of our different beliefs. There were often some tense discussions, but we came to agreement on how we would present our two traditions and belief systems to the children, and now we both make efforts to present a unified front of respect and understanding for each other to the kids."

HOW TO DEAL WITH CAREER CHALLENGES, CHANGES, AND SETBACKS

"If one of you has suffered a career setback, it isn't the end of the world. You are a team, so focus on helping each other through this time. If it's necessary to keep your finances afloat, a stay-at-home parent could get a part-time job or the working spouse could temporarily take on a second job. The most important thing is to stay positive and support one another through these tough times."

"At some point one of you may decide to make a major career change—for instance, entering a whole new field, going back to school, or starting your own business. To avoid resentment on either of your parts, map out a tangible 'dreams made real' deal with your spouse that balances sacrifice and personal fulfillment for both of you. In other words, make sure that one of you is not doing all the sacrificing. I'm living this situation, and yes, there are moments of panic and doom and 'why was it that I didn't marry a Rockefeller'? But making sacrifices you both agree on to achieve a goal is far less stressful than living with a miserable, overworked, job-hating spouse."

"When one of you is out of work, due either to quitting a job or to getting fired, it may seem like a setback, but it's actually a great time to explore new hobbies: golfing, painting, or anything that you've always been curious about but have never had time to try. It might feel extravagant, but just remember that you are investing in yourself by learning something new that relaxes you. This will also take some of the pressure off the working spouse, who may feel guilty about having a job when the other doesn't."

"Because our identity is formed partly by the work we do, when we lose or change jobs, it can take a toll on our self-esteem. My husband had a tough time after he was laid off, but we realized that it was a great opportunity for him to reinvent himself. He thought of other fields that could use his talents and found the new job search an exciting challenge."

"There may come a time when one of you puts your career growth and dreams on hold—for instance, one stays in an unfulfilling but stable job so the other can build a business, go to school, or even stay home with the kids for a while. The one doing the sacrificing should be recognized and complimented regularly. It goes a long way to hear, 'I appreciate what you're doing,' or, 'You are amazing,' or whatever the appropriate kudos for the situation are."

WHEN YOU NEED COUPLES THERAPY

"Sometimes marriage can be more stressful than rewarding. When the stress gets to be too much and you feel like your spouse isn't respecting your feelings, it's time to get help. Don't just throw in the towel, and don't be afraid to ask your spouse to get help with you. If you are feeling overwhelmed or unloved, have faith that those feelings will pass—if you both deal with the situation. Remember that sometimes it's much easier (and more satisfying) to fix a broken relationship than it is to start a new one."

"Going to couples therapy doesn't necessarily mean that your marriage is in trouble. But if there are particular communication problems you'd like to work through, having a neutral listener might be a good idea. Then you can take the tips you've learned in counseling and apply them on your own."

"My husband became verbally abusive to me in front of the kids, which made me very unhappy and made me want to leave him. It meant a lot that he was willing to see a therapist with me about his behavior, and it inspired me not to give up on our marriage."

"*If* you and your husband have reached an insurmountable roadblock in your marriage, it's time to do something. Do you love each other? Do you want to stay together? Do you care about each other's happiness? Then do something about it. If you can't resolve things yourselves, bring in a third party or you can expect the troubles to continue — and more serious ones to arise."

"*It* takes two people to create conflict in a marriage, and that means you have to resolve the problems together as well. Go with an open mind to a couples counselor, and you might be surprised at the results; talking about things rather than bottling them up will help a lot. My husband and I came close to splitting up, and at that point we realized we needed outside intervention. It was hard to do, but couples therapy has helped us both mature. Sometimes we didn't think we could make it, but we have, and we're glad that we took the necessary steps to keep our marriage going."

ADDRESS LIFE'S CHALLENGES AS A TEAM

"Don't let the upheavals life presents stop you in your tracks. Whatever the cause, know that you can adjust as long as you face the challenge together. Talk about your fears and concerns and the general quality of your lifestyle. It's important to keep your perspective, to remember the big picture. No matter where you are or what your situation is, think of how much your marriage means to you both. In the long run, setbacks might bring you closer."

"My husband and I have always lived in the town where I grew up. Recently, for various reasons, we began to contemplate a move, which would be a major transition for our family. But my husband has been willing to sit down with me and talk, plan, and ponder all of the potential problems, as well as the positive aspects this change will bring. That has made all the difference. He has helped me to see the benefits of making a big transition and has patiently listened to my concerns. He also sat down with our children and explained to them the positive aspects of living in a new city. Having that kind of support at this critical juncture has made us both stronger and has allowed us to view life as an adventure to navigate together—which makes it exciting rather than scary. It has been great to have my spouse's reassurance and support at such an important time."

"*W*hen you have to make a big life change, it's more important than ever to show your support for each other. Let your spouse know that you still need him. Make gestures, large and small, to let him know that your bond is still a crucial one."

"*S*taying married when your child is critically ill requires a conscious decision to take the hard road. Relationships for those of us in these situations can mean giving the other person a listening ear when you are dead-on-your-feet-tired and ready to drop, doing all the work at home so the other parent can sit in the hospital, and bending gender roles and responsibilities. For a marriage to work in this situation, you need to support each other at all times. I don't mean you don't fight, but the underlying belief has to be, 'It's us against the world.'"

"My husband and I moved across the country because of his job change. Then his company went bankrupt and he found a good job in yet another state, leaving the kids and me behind until I could find something and join him—even though I had already settled into a stable job. He'd tried to stay where we were but could not. I finally realized that the right thing to do was keep our family together in the same place, and that meant making a sacrifice to move to a new city again. It was scary, but I'm glad I did it. My husband has agreed that he'll do the same thing for me if a great job opportunity comes up for me at some point."

CHAPTER 4

How to Deal with Money as a Couple

⁓

"*E*ven though we are financially stable right now, I've always let my husband know that if it all went away tomorrow, we would be fine. We talk about the possibility of having less money, but I always drive home the point that whatever happens, it's not the end of the world. We don't fight about money because we plan things together and reassure each other when one of us is concerned about it. Having money is not as important to us as having good health or a happy family. "

LEARN TO TALK ABOUT MONEY WITHOUT FIGHTING

"My husband and I have had lots of conversations about money and how to handle it. We both tend to be spenders rather than savers, so we've had to work on that together. The most important thing, like in many aspects of marriage, is communication and the willingness to compromise."

"*D*eal with the subject of money before it can turn into a problem, even if it's a hard issue to bring up. The more you talk about it, the less you have to worry about it later."

"*I*f one (or both) of you is lashing out during a discussion of family finances, it might be a sign that there's some insecurity about money. You may need to convince each other that money is an issue for you both, rather than something that only one of you is responsible for. Remind yourselves that you're in it together and that two heads are better than one in sorting through money issues."

"Fortunately my husband and I entered into our marriage with similar ideas about money management. Our families also have similar attitudes toward money, so there wasn't too much adaptation needed. However, one difficult area for us to negotiate has been the timing of expenses. Rather than argue about who is right, we have compromised. That way, if I want to buy a new car, for instance, my husband doesn't just rule it out. Instead we sit down with a calendar and talk about the best timing for a major new purchase. We make sure that we're both comfortable with it so there is no resentment. We don't always agree, but what matters is that we have found a way to talk about money in a productive way."

"*F*inancial issues are often what break up a
marriage, so it's especially important to talk about
money in a productive, honest way. Be as blunt
and open with each other as you can so that there
is no hidden resentment about how your money is
being spent. If one of you is unhappy about the
way money is handled in your household, deal with
it immediately. Of course you should always be
tactful, but you should also be able to freely
discuss your concerns. Don't keep any anxieties to
yourself because that won't help either of you.
Remember that you're a team."

SET GUIDELINES ON HOW TO MANAGE MONEY

"Since we bought a computer, my husband and I have done a much better job of tracking our spending. We were shocked to learn where our money was going. Spending is a hard habit to break, but each year we are doing better. We monitor our money more closely, keep good records on the computer, and are both careful not to buy frivolous things too often. More than once we have stopped each other from buying something we'd regret later on!"

"My husband and I used to have significant money issues, but we have worked through them. He had a lot of debt, and although I didn't want to tell him how to spend his money, I also didn't want debt to be a huge part of our lives. We had a serious talk about his spending and set some new guidelines. Now we are both saving for home ownership and investing for retirement. As long as we do that and pay our bills, we each have some wiggle room in the budget so that we can use the remaining amount from our paychecks to do whatever we want."

"We have three accounts: our joint account, mine, and his. Our paychecks are deposited right into our joint account. Then I pay the bills. Then he transfers money into our separate accounts. This way the bills get paid, but we also get to save money or spend money—the choice is ours. So we help each other but also give each other the freedom to do things separately without resenting one another."

"When there are no specific guidelines in a marriage for spending money and one person has an overspending problem, the end result is that your marriage may be destroyed. The first step is to admit that there is a problem with money. Then, together, you can decide on a solution. If the problems are serious and ongoing, you may even want to contemplate counseling to set financial guidelines."

"Create a list of where the money has to go each month—mortgage, car payments, credit cards, savings, children's education, and so on—so that you are both aware of exactly how high your bills are. Then make a budget together that provides 'fun' money for both of you, pin it to the refrigerator, and check off bills when you pay them so that you both know which ones have been taken care of and which ones are to come."

IDENTIFY WHO WILL BE THE HOUSEHOLD CFO

"Since I'm better at handling money than my husband is, I was appointed to be in charge of family finances. Neither of us is good about writing down what we have spent, so I created a plan to make us see how much we spend and stick to our budget. We have five envelopes: His Weekly; My Weekly; Grocery; Weekend Spending; Emergency. At the beginning of each week, I put money into each envelope. If either of us spends a large portion of our money early in the week by buying lunches or going out at night, this forces us to bring our lunches to work the rest of the week or cut back somewhere else. It's strict, but it works."

"My husband used to hide bills from me, and he wouldn't ask for help if he fell behind in payments. Finally I took over managing the finances myself, which wasn't easy for him to accept at first. Now we have a system: I tell him what I paid toward bills each month and how much he owes me, and he writes me a check. This has turned into an efficient arrangement that works well for both of us."

"Be honest with each other about who is better at handling money, and don't be threatened by the answer. If your husband is the better CFO, let him do the job — keeping you informed of what's going on, of course, since you're a team. What matters most is that the bills get paid on time, not who does it."

"My husband and I have consolidated everything into joint accounts. We consider everything in our marriage as one unit, and we like to make all financial decisions together so that there is no division of 'mine' and 'yours.' Sharing in the managing of our finances has worked well, although that might not be the best solution for everyone. We evenly divide paying bills each month and always keep the other person updated on what's been done."

"We've found that I'm actually better at doing the bills than my husband is. Though it's a big task on my part and I don't necessarily enjoy it, it seems to work. He wasn't exactly happy about all of it in the beginning, but when he realized that it's just one less chore he has to do, he was happy to hand over checks to me and let me figure out how to disperse them! Every once in a while he decides he's going to take care of the bills as they come in, but otherwise they're my job."

DEAL WITH DIFFERENCES IN EARNING POWER

"My husband had a sudden downturn in his income level, which can be a devastating blow to some men's self-esteem. Many men seem to base their self-worth on how much they earn. I found that reassuring him about all the other qualities I love about him was very helpful. I also reminded him that any money coming into the house was always for both of us, regardless of who earned it."

"Even though there may be a difference in a couple's earning power, are you both willing to work as a marital team? If you both contribute whatever amount you can toward monthly household expenses and savings, neither person should resent the other. By respecting what you both have to contribute and being open about it, you'll be able to avoid conflicts about money."

"I had to put a stop to the competitiveness my husband was showing about our salaries. It took him a while to understand that we were together as one and that he shouldn't think about earnings as his versus mine. I earn less than he does and asked him to consider how he'd feel if he were in my shoes. After we talked about it, I stopped feeling inadequate and we were able to get past it."

"*If* you are a stay-at-home or part-time working spouse and your husband brings in the income but complains that you're not 'pulling your weight' financially, you might want to remind him of your value around the home — doing the laundry, cooking, and housecleaning! The work women do around the house is 'unseen' labor and is often taken for granted. Offering to stop doing the household chores for a while might remind your husband about the value of what you contribute."

"My husband earns considerably more money than I do, yet I am more than happy to keep our checking accounts separate. I've always been independent, and I like the idea that I take care of my own credit card debt and other personal bills. Of course, I can always go to my husband for help if I need it, and we do have a joint savings account—which we set up to provide for the other if one of us died prematurely or became seriously ill. He puts in more money than I do every month, but I've learned to feel okay about that by taking care of my own day-to-day expenses. Handling money as a couple can often become a power issue, one that I wanted to avoid. This arrangement has worked out well and has ensured that neither of us feels resentment toward the other about how much money we earn."

DETERMINE YOUR FINANCIAL GOALS AS A COUPLE

"Start thinking now about your financial goals: Do you have enough money to have children? If you have children, have you started saving for their college education? Would you like to own a home someday? It's never too soon to start saving in order to achieve your goals. First, though, you should work on having a six months' cash emergency fund, in case one of you loses a job. Unemployment can happen to anyone, and savings will cause less of a strain if you are forced to live on one income for a while."

"My husband and I came up with a general plan for when we would have children, and I immediately began putting away $200 a month in savings. I didn't want to be at home with the kids and be sad about not having enough money. When we did have children, I had all that money saved up for trips to the zoo, dining out, and family vacations—things we would have just done without. So it's a good idea to figure out a plan that you can start now, one that will make things easier for you later on; you'll have money readily available to you when you need it."

"Goal setting is an ongoing conversation for us. My husband and I constantly ask each other if a purchase is really necessary or if it will help us down the road. When it comes to making one goal a priority over another, we figure out what would be most meaningful to both of us. We discuss what we both want to do—not just one person's goals—and decide what can be realistically accomplished."

"We handle goal setting efficiently in my household. Our immediate goals (about six months or so ahead) are posted next to the computer so we see them each time we balance our checking account. Because my husband is more of a spender than I am, writing down our goals has helped him stick to our budget and see how satisfying it is to accomplish each goal by saving for it."

"My husband and I have been able to easily establish our long-term goals, such as retirement and saving for our children's college fund. We feel lucky to have similar ideas about how we'd like to spend our money. The tricky aspect was how to go about it and stick to our financial goals. My attitude has always been that I work hard for my money, so I should have fun and enjoy it; my husband feels the same way to an extent, but he has shown me how nice it feels to watch a savings account build up over time. That has had a great influence on me, so now we are both equally committed to putting away a certain amount of each paycheck every month and seeing how quickly our savings can grow."

CHAPTER 5

How to Live Together Happily—Forever

~

"What you put into a marriage is as rewarding as what you get out of it, so never take each other for granted. Make every day count. Remind yourselves why you fell in love in the first place, no matter how many years go by. And never stop having new adventures together."

Remember, Two Halves Make a Whole

"If you don't look for your spouse's strengths and how they complement yours, what you will see is each other's failings, and you will miss out on how you can work together. Early on, we'd get into arguments about why one wasn't doing what the other was in various situations, until we realized that we were better off dividing and conquering. For instance, I'm much better at staying in touch with people and planning events than my husband is. He, however, is much better at being relaxed and jovial when we have people over. So together we come off as great hosts, where as individually we'd each have our failings."

"I tend to be focused on building and maintaining a happy, healthy relationship in very by-the-book ways (being romantic, showing your love, expressing yourself, and so on). My husband's strength is his ability to be silly and find humor even in the most annoying or sad situations. He can make a joke of a stupid fight we're having, for example, and it does help defuse the anger. Putting both approaches together helps keep our marriage healthy—my way tends to keep us on an even keel day-to-day, while his pulls us out of stormy weather."

"In our marriage, I tend to be the more idealistic one, more of a dreamer. I tend to make our adventures, such as a weekend getaway, happen. My husband is more pragmatic and even cynical, so he keeps me grounded. He thinks about things that don't cross my mind and uses common sense at times when I might not. Sometimes I wish he'd be more carefree, but I do think we manage to strike a healthy balance."

"My husband and I are both quite outgoing and friendly. However, we each deal better with different kinds of people. My husband is more of a 'good ol' boy' type; he always hits it off with older people and gets a cheaper deal on car repairs. I'm better with 'prissy' people—uptight bank officers and other nose-in-the-air types. I'm more willing to play the game to get what I want, while he can't tolerate it."

"*I* used to think that in order for a marriage to work, a couple has to share exactly the same character traits. That was, until I met my husband. We're polar opposites. He's concrete; I'm abstract. He's quiet; I'm talkative. He's messy but always knows where his stuff is; I'm neat but am always losing things. About the only thing we had in common when we got married was our love for each other and the fact we both knew we wanted children. Now I know it's the differences that make our marriage so interesting—how boring it would be if we liked the exact same things all the time, were always in agreement with each other, and never brought anything new to the table. As long as a couple shares the same basic goals, opposites can make a marriage work."

LEARN TO DEAL WITH EACH OTHER'S FAMILIES

"My husband and I had some in-law problems that took a few years to settle. His parents would often drop by unannounced, even after we told them it wasn't a good time. I became frustrated and was tired of my husband making me feel like the bad guy. Thankfully, we have established some good boundaries now. My husband and I agreed to establish regular visiting days for them and to be firm about it. That way, they come over only when they're invited, and it's worked out great. I don't get stressed out around them and actually enjoy our time together."

"Don't whine and complain to your family about your spouse on a regular basis. Keep in mind that your family (and friends) will always—or at least usually—side with you even when you're wrong. If you constantly complain about your spouse to your family and friends, they will start to dislike him, which will cause you all sorts of difficulties later."

"My husband was married once before, and his ex-wife did some serious emotional damage to his parents as well as him. I try to go the extra mile with both his father and mother to make sure they know that I am not the first wife. There are times when I know his mom is uncomfortable, making me apprehensive that I did something to trigger a past-experience response, but over time things are getting better."

"My husband and my parents just do not get along; I guess it's simply a matter of clashing personalities. When he told me that he didn't want to constantly spend time with them when they visited, I was very hurt. Eventually I realized that he was just trying to be honest with me and that having fewer, shorter visits of quality time together was better than having him sulk and be unhappy around them. Now when they come to see us, he will join us for part of the time and go off with his friends for the rest. I actually think he has a much healthier relationship with my parents now."

"My in-laws are terrific, and most of the time we get along really well. But there have been times when they made me feel really angry or hurt. When that happens, I force myself to get on the phone with them and try to have a normal conversation about something else, just so I don't start brooding about the situation. In my own family people stopped talking when they got mad—sometimes they didn't talk again for months (and in a few cases, they stopped talking for good). As a kid I thought this was really silly, so I try to remember how I felt then. There have been times when I have been so angry with my husband's sister that I never wanted to talk to her again, but those are the times when I know I need to get a grip, phone her, and break the ice."

NEGOTIATE HOUSEHOLD TASKS

"My husband tends to help with chores when I ask him to but otherwise forgets. He just doesn't notice if things are untidy. Rather than sulk about it, I've learned to ask him directly for help and have assigned him certain tasks to do on his own, such as mowing the lawn, hauling out garbage, and fixing whatever breaks—things I'm just not good at doing. Even though he isn't a self-starter when it comes to chores, I really appreciate that he tries to do his equal share around the house, rather than leaving it all to me."

"I used to keep score about who did what around my house, but I don't do that any more. When I really think about it, my husband helps out a lot. Recently we decided to divide up our chores, and the list seems evenly distributed. I do most of the cleaning, cooking, and laundry; my husband keeps our house in good repair, pays our bills, and does the yard work — except weeding, after he 'weeded' some of my flowers."

"When I first got married, I found that I was doing almost everything that needed to be done around the house. Finally I sat down and wrote out a list of what I did and what my husband did, and I showed it to him. He couldn't believe it; he had a very different perception of his contributions. That list opened up a dialogue about the issue, and we were able to split up the tasks in a way that seemed fair to both of us."

"Luckily my husband and I have established who should do what in our household so that neither of us does all the work alone. And it just so happens that we both manage to avoid the tasks we dislike or aren't good at: I would never let my husband do the laundry, for example, because I know how to do it right and like doing it. My husband happens to enjoy ironing and is much better at it than I am. Some things we both like to do, such as cooking together and working in our garden. We've worked out a very good system for ourselves."

"In the first few years of my marriage, I somehow found myself buying presents—for birthdays, weddings, holiday parties, everything—for all of my husband's relatives (often people I didn't know that well). My husband would then complain about what I'd bought! So I told my husband that I couldn't handle the stress any more and that he needed to take on the gift-buying responsibilities for his family. He handled the news surprisingly well, probably because I emphasized that I adored his relatives and that this wasn't a reflection of how I felt about them. I also let him know that I was happy to pitch in as backup any time, but I couldn't be responsible for keeping track of gifts and cards for his family on top of mine."

LEARN TO UNDERSTAND EACH OTHER'S MOODS

"Early in my marriage, I wasn't always sure how to deal with my husband's moods. If something bothered him, he often preferred not to discuss it. For instance, if it were late in the evening, he would just go to sleep. Since I have never been able to fall asleep angry, this difference used to bother me. I came to realize that he's not always angry; he just can't deal with the issue that day, and a good night's sleep is simply what he needs to tackle it."

"A lot of dealing with your partner's mood is having a sense of timing. I would never approach my husband about a heated topic if he hasn't had much sleep or if he's walking out the door. He knows not to approach me while I'm dealing with the kids or feeling cranky due to 'that time of the month.' It takes understanding on both sides, but it works."

"It would be nice, of course, if couples could read each other perfectly in every situation—there would be no miscommunications or misunderstandings. But that just doesn't happen. So sometimes, if you're not sure what your spouse is thinking, it's good to just ask him, 'Are you okay?' It's a matter of being sensitive about where the other person's head is at the moment—and if you are not sure, just ask, and go from there."

"*I'm* fortunate that my husband is wonderfully intuitive and sensitive. I am the sort of person who is in a good mood the majority of the time, but when I am not, he usually knows and understands. He is always good about staying calm and reassuring me. When it comes to his moods, however, I had to learn to accept the way that he gets quiet and introverted (very unlike how he usually behaves) when something is bothering him. In the very early stages of our relationship, I would get hysterical and try to force him to talk, thinking it was something about me. Now I feel much more secure and relaxed and have realized that most of the time he is thinking about something that has nothing to do with me, so I give him space unless he comes to me with a problem."

"It took me a long time to understand that just because my husband was upset about something, he wasn't necessarily upset with me. The fact is, I initiated more than one fight because I thought whatever was making him moody and grumpy had to be something I did and I nagged him about it until I did become what was ticking him off. I've learned not to push him when he's a bit withdrawn, and he's gotten better about telling me that he does have something (work, his family, whatever) on his mind and reassuring me that it's not something I did."

GET PAST EACH OTHER'S ANNOYING LITTLE HABITS

"Learn to separate genuine relationship issues from trivial annoyances that occur daily. Some things are worth talking about, but others you will have to learn to live with, so don't dwell on everything. If he leaves the toilet seat up no matter how many times you tell him not to, you might have to let go of that issue and remind yourself that you probably have habits that annoy your husband, too."

"My husband would always let the toilet paper run out and never buy more, and for some reason this little habit made me very upset. I solved the problem by not buying more, rather than coming to the rescue. My husband picked up the hint and is now very good at buying the toilet paper for our household. Since that happened, I asked him to tell me about one habit of mine that he would like me to change, which I did. As long as you have a lot of respect for your spouse, you can deal with each other's habits in a productive way and not let them turn into major issues."

"*I* used to be driven crazy by my husband's habit of telling me how to drive. I got past it by often choosing to drive alone on errands we used to go on together (such as grocery shopping). Also, I started doing the same thing to him when he drove, and he admitted it was pretty annoying! That has taken care of it."

"*My* husband and I have always gotten along well and never really argued. It was the little things that used to annoy us, habits that were incompatible. I think we both used to get worked up about those minor things. Yet once we had children, we somehow got past being annoyed about each other's habits—we were simply too busy and tired to keep paying attention to things that didn't really matter. That was one of the great gifts our kids gave us—a better perspective on what is truly important in life."

"My husband has always been horrible about picking things up, taking care of the house, and being considerate about tidiness. I think this is because his mother always did everything for him. When I was single, I used to be kind of compulsive about stuff having a place and being kept there, but having him around forced me to choose between loosening up and losing my mind. I still pester him sometimes, but I've learned to relax a bit and not let everything get to me. When you live with someone, you have to live with his habits as well. Some you just have to accept, especially the ones that really have no impact on the happiness of your relationship."

LEAVE ROOM IN YOUR LIVES FOR FRIENDS

"My husband and I both have our friends; some we have made as a couple, others are individual friends. Knowing that our partner is able to relax and have a good time with others isn't threatening to either of us. I have a standing monthly lunch date with a number of friends, and my husband looks forward to doing special projects with the kids while I'm out. He's got his amateur radio club and enjoys spending time with those buddies. Everyone needs some time when they can just be themselves—not someone's spouse or someone's parent, but a person in their own right."

"*F*inding a balance between having independence and staying connected with your spouse is a tricky thing; there's no answer that works for every couple. My husband and I are extremely close, but we both like to spend time with our friends. We keep a bulletin board with our schedules posted on it and never make plans on nights we have reserved as 'date nights' just for us. We communicate regularly about what's happening in our social lives so that one of us isn't always out having a good time while the other one sits lonely at home. The nice thing is that we have many friends in common and love having dinner parties in our home. On the other hand, my husband is grateful that I have friends who love to go shopping with me so he can be excused from that duty."

"Recently I realized that I hardly ever made plans with my friends anymore. So I decided that I was taking a weekend off. I went away with my best friends and had a great time. My husband was uncomfortable about my spending a whole weekend away from the family, but after I returned home in such a happy mood, he understood this was a good idea and has encouraged me to connect with my friends more often."

"Our family moved to a new city last year, and both my husband and I found the idea of making new friends somewhat daunting. One of the things we did was take a class in ballroom dancing, and we met some wonderful people there who made our adjustment to a new city much easier. Having made the leap, not only have my husband and I formed good friendships, but we've also acquired new hobbies that have enriched our lives."

"For a long time my husband and I did everything together, which was great but also problematic. I really wanted to nurture the friendships I'd let slip away, so I started to make regular 'girls' night out' dates and had the time of my life reconnecting with friends. My husband told me my behavior seemed inappropriate because I was spending more time away from him. I knew that I was doing nothing wrong but understood that he was reacting this way because he felt insecure. It was a new thing for both of us, and he is more introverted in general. We worked through this issue slowly: I encouraged him to pursue his own interests and to have an occasional 'boys' night out.' I also emphasized that although we needed to have some separate friends, it didn't represent a void in our marriage. When my husband understood that he was still my top priority and that I was trying to be sensitive to his feelings, he accepted what I was saying."

GIVE EACH OTHER ROOM TO GROW

"My husband has a part-time job as a drummer in a band, playing regular gigs in a nearby town. When I became pregnant, he seemed stressed out every time he told me that he was going to meet his band. Of course it wasn't ideal that he had practice four days a week, but music is a passionate interest of his, and his band is starting to take off. I wasn't going to take that away from him and explained to him that it was fine. I think having individual interests and hobbies only enhances a marriage, even if it means making some compromises."

"Thanks to my husband's support, a hobby that I was introduced to—computers—is now my full-time job. Without his encouragement and help, I would have never taken the first steps toward that area. I've come a long way from who I was five years ago, when I couldn't even boot up a computer on my own! In the beginning my husband was completely involved in helping me learn the skills I needed to get comfortable with computers; now he's content to sit on the sidelines. Of course I also offer support on things he is involved in; I've helped him at work and have encouraged him to pursue his dream of owning his own business. Every dream or goal each of us reaches only enriches our lives together."

"*A* few years ago I learned a valuable life lesson: When I do things just for me and take time out for myself, I am a better mother and wife and a more generous friend. I like taking long hot baths, spending time with a good book—whatever I feel I need—usually on weekends. My husband and I will take turns playing with the kids while the other person has some pampering time; for my husband that means playing sports or fishing. We know we need that private time to grow, and we're good about seeing that we both get it. "

"My husband is not a very ambitious guy, which was never an issue for me until I decided to go to law school. I received many scholarship offers and did not want to turn down this opportunity. For some reason, however, my husband found this new path threatening, which only made me feel resentful—I felt like he was holding me back. We went to see a couples therapist for a few months to resolve this issue. Because he is not ambitious, it was hard for him to understand that law school was just something I had to do for myself, to follow my dream, and that it wouldn't have a negative effect on our family. I know I made the right decision in getting this degree, and now I feel even better about it after getting my husband's full support."

$\mathcal{P}$LAN YOUR LIFE TOGETHER

"$\mathcal{W}$hen we got married, my husband and I planned all the usual basics: home ownership, children, careers. Recently, though, we have been planning for our eventual retirement. Although it is many years away, we've enjoyed dreaming about our old age together! We're saving money in our pension plans at work, and when we retire, we've decided that we'll buy a Winnebago and do a lot of traveling around the U.S. and Canada, which seems very romantic."

"*E*arly in our marriage, my husband and I established
what our 'needs' were and what our 'wants' were. And
we planned how we were going to satisfy both. A few of
our long-term goals are going to be costly, so we're both
socking away large amounts of money in investments.
Doing it together, our dreams actually seem like
possibilities. Even if they don't work out, we'll be there
to help each other out."

"*T*o live happily ever after, I think you need to have
shared life goals. Every New Year's Eve my husband
and I write down our hopes for the new year in a book
and share them with each other. At the very least, it
keeps you communicating about what you want (learn
wines!) so there aren't surprises ('Oh, you want a new
kitchen?'). At the very best, you wind up having a much
more exciting, fully realized life together."

"My husband and I got stressed out talking about all the things we wanted to achieve in life, together and in our careers. We felt paralyzed by wanting to accomplish so much. When we got out some paper and actually wrote down our goals, we realized that we could compromise on some and focus on others. Keeping a list of our life plans has helped us because we also saw that we want the same things and have similar values, and that was very comforting. I have no trouble envisioning our future decades from now, and I see us as compatible in the future as we are today."

"I think it's easy for couples to forget how talking about their hopes and dreams impacts their relationship. When we're all first in love, we talk to each other about what we hope for in our homes and children and lives, but then so often, we get busy making those things happen and stop looking toward the future. And then people get frustrated and ask, 'Is this all there is?' I think continually talking about your life goals with your spouse is powerfully romantic, and always keeping an eye on the future helps keep a relationship alive."

ABOUT STACIA RAGOLIA

Stacia Ragolia is the vice president of community and services at iVillage. She and her family live in Westchester County, New York.

ABOUT iVILLAGE

Based in New York City, iVillage Inc. was founded in 1995 with the intention of "humanizing cyberspace." In the early years of the Internet, there were few places for women to find solutions and discuss their problems, needs, and interests. By providing a clean, well-lit space, iVillage carved out a unique place where women could gather and find information and support on a wide range of topics relevant to their lives.

Today, iVillage is a leading women's media company and the number one source for women's information online, providing practical solutions and everyday support for women. iVillage includes iVillage.com, Women.com, Business Women's Network, Lamaze Publishing, the Newborn Channel, iVillage UK, Promotions.com, and Astrology.com.

iVillage.com's content areas include Astrology, Babies, Beauty, Diet & Fitness, Entertainment, Food, Health, Home & Garden, Lamaze, Money, Parenting, Pets, Pregnancy, Relationships, Shopping, and Work.

WHAT'S YOUR BEST ADVICE?

iVillage has always believed that many of the best solutions for problems in women's lives come from other women who've "been there and *solved* that." We invite you to become part of our network of advice-giving women and to have your words of wisdom featured in upcoming iVillage Solutions books. Send your best advice on dating and marriage to iVillage Solutions Books, iVillage Inc., 512 Seventh Avenue, New York, NY 10018. Or write us by email at ivillagesolutionsbooks@mail.ivillage.com.

We look forward to hearing your advice, as well as any of your comments and thoughts about our books.